I0901593

IMAGES
of America

CLEVELAND COUNTY FAIR

On the Cover: Miss America Maria Beale Fletcher clutches her crown while she and her escort enjoy a ride at the Cleveland County Fair in 1962. (Courtesy of the Cleveland County Fair Association Archives.)

IMAGES
of America

CLEVELAND COUNTY FAIR

Marie Farrow Patterson and
U.L. "Rusty" Patterson

ARCADIA
PUBLISHING

ISBN 978-0-7385-9246-6

Published by Arcadia Publishing
Charleston, South Carolina

Printed in the United States of America

Library of Congress Control Number: 2011944464

For all general information, please contact Arcadia Publishing:
Telephone 843-853-2070
Fax 843-853-0044
E-mail sales@arcadiapublishing.com
For customer service and orders:
Toll-Free 1-888-313-2665

Visit us on the Internet at www.arcadiapublishing.com

This book is dedicated to the memory of
Dr. Barry E. Hambright,
historian, author, and friend.

Contents

ACKNOWLEDGMENTS

The authors wish to thank those who have helped make this publication possible. Many people throughout the county have graciously and enthusiastically provided photographs, names, and background information. Most images are from the Cleveland County Fair Association Archives. Credit has been given at the end of each caption for photographs from other collections. Several publications have been instrumental confirming people, names, facts, and timelines, including the following: *History of the Cleveland County Fair* by Grace Hamrick; *The Living Past of Cleveland County* by Lee B. Weathers; the Shelby newspaper, the *Star*; and *Meet Me at the Waterwheel*, a video history produced by Mary Lopez. The works of professional photographers Floyd Willis, the Ellis Studio, and the Lloyd Hamrick Collection have been instrumental in developing the book.

We are grateful to Calvin Hastings, Andy Elmore, Robert Arey, Mrs. J. Sib Dorton Jr., Phillip Glover, Scott Glover, Brett Elliott, Margaret Patterson, George Hamrick, Margaret Yarboro, David Beam, Randy Sweeting, Shane Combs, Roby Combs, Tommy Forney, Edwin Ford, Charles Webb, Howard Scruggs, Raymond Sams, Ambrose Cline, Jean Poston Cline, Katherine Panther-Potemkin, the Jack Morgan family, Marion Lee, Wanda Webber, Judy Brown, Becky Dellinger, Kent Bridges, Jane C. Green, and Tommy Greene for their contributions of photographs and histories. Personal interviews with the late Joe A. Goforth proved invaluable to writing the history of the Cleveland County Fair.

A reasonable effort has been made to gather accurate information about each image. All of these people helped to make this publication possible. None of them are responsible for the errors, which are the authors' alone.

Introduction

In the fall of 1923, members of the Shelby Kiwanis Club began developing a plan to create a county-wide fair, combining the Boiling Springs Community Fair, the Fallston Community Fair, and the Union Community Fair into one event. The civic club initiated a fundraising effort with Cleveland County Fair Night on January 24, 1924. Through the sale of $20 shares of stock, the Shelby Kiwanis raised $15,000 to establish the fair. The first Cleveland County Fair was held October 14–18, 1924, with a reported 70,000 in attendance.

The fair quickly became a regional event and was billed as the largest agricultural county fair in North Carolina. Among the first officers of the fair association was local veterinarian Dr. J.S. Dorton, who went on to manage the fair for 38 years. "Doc," as he was known, said, "The purpose of the fair is to provide an opportunity for citizens to display the fruits of their labors, to meet and compare notes on crops, livestock, farm machinery, home development and improvement."

While the excitement of the carnival rides and auto races proved crucial to the early success of the fair, it is important to recognize the impact Dr. J.S. Dorton and the county fair has had on the economic development of Cleveland County. Doc had an unwavering commitment to bringing the best agriculture practices to Cleveland County. The fair attracted the best in cattle from top cattle-raising regions in the nation to be exhibited locally. Clevelanders saw firsthand what was possible in the industry, and their efforts paid off. Through the years, the fair sponsored the Better Acres Program, Dream Farm Exhibits, 4-H competitions, Boy Scout and Girl Scout exhibits, home demonstrations, public school booths, Future Homemakers of America, and Future Farmers of America.

Doc's formula for a successful fair included the bringing together of farm and city life to showcase agriculture and industry with exhibits and education. Added to the mix were carnival rides and games and entertainment on the grandstand. Throughout the years, the ingredients have changed, but the formula for a successful fair remains the same.

The first chapter shows a compilation of photographs from the first 35 years of the fair; there is no timeline, as images of the fair before 1938 are very rare. The following chapters unveil the formula for success of the largest agricultural county fair in North Carolina.

One

The Formula for Success

This image from 1903 depicts a community carnival in uptown Shelby. The original courthouse on the square is visible to the left, and the original Methodist church is to the right. Before 1924, community fairs were held throughout the county in Boiling Springs, Patterson Springs, and the Union Community. (Courtesy of the *Highlander*.)

In the first quarter of the 20th century, much of Cleveland County was made up of rural farmland. Small family farms were found throughout the county. Families grew crops and raised livestock to support their needs. Joe and Eula Bailey posed with their grandchildren on their farm in western Cleveland County for this photograph. (Courtesy of Joe Ellis.)

The Tomato Club in Belwood is recognized as the first organization of agriculture extension in Cleveland County. Pictured from left to right in this 1915 photograph are Hattie Bingham, Ora Sain, Carrie Willis, Jettie Hicks, and Susan Elliott Weathers, the county's first home demonstration agent. (Courtesy of the Cleveland County Agriculture Extension.)

Agriculture extension agents went to the fields to meet with farmers to discuss improvements in seeds, fertilizer, and growing practices. Area farmers were industrious, thrifty, and ready to accept improved farming methods. Agriculture agents taught such things as the chemistry of the soil, the necessity for using commercial fertilizer and pedigreed seed, terracing the fields to prevent soil erosion, and the benefit of crop rotation. (Courtesy of the Jack Morgan family.)

O.Z. Morgan, a pioneer in agriculture extension in Cleveland County and North Carolina, poses with John D. Honeycutt and R.P. Weathers while examining a Cleveland County cotton field. By the 1920s, cotton was becoming the crop of choice to grow. By the 1930s, Cleveland County led the state of North Carolina in yield per acre for cotton produced. (Courtesy of the Jack Morgan family.)

THE HIGHLANDER

AND SHELBY NEWS

75,000 POPULATION

Cleveland County Fair Association Organizes

EXPERT EMPLOYED TO SUPERINTEND WORK AT FAIR GROUNDS

$5,000 Needed to Complete the Work and You Are Invited to Send in Your Contribution.

GET IN BEHIND THE FAIR AND PUT IT OVER.

Listen fellows, the Fair Association needs about $5,000 cash or in other words subscriptions to that amount to put it over as it should be and there **is nothing to do but to raise it.**

Cleveland has a reputation to sustain in this matter. Go where you will throughout the North State and the fame of this fine old county greets you, and naturally we are proud of it. Cleveland has the reputation of going after the thing that she wants and the general impression is that she usually lands, which is correct.

Several of the enterprising citizens of the county have banded themselves into a body to solicit and to work, in other ways, as well as subscribe liberally, to the cause, but we **can't expect them to do it all.** They have raised fully two-thirds of the amount and now it is up to the rank and file to get busy. It is a physical impossibility to see every man in the county so in order to get it before the people The Highlander is printing a blank below that you can mail in if you haven't the time to come to town.

Don't be bashful, fill it out and mail it to Dr. J. S. Dorton, Shelby, N. C., and you will not only be helping a good cause now, but you will be building for the future an institution that will be of benefit to not only your children, but your children's children.

Do it now before you forget it. Sign it with pencil or pen and small contributions will be appreciated same as the larger ones. Here's our hand neighbor, make it a hundred or five and thank your stars that you had the opportunity to help.

SUPERIOR COURT CONVENES ON NEXT MONDAY

LADIES' NIGHT A BIG SUCCESS

CHIMNEY ROCK SURVEY FINISHED

At a meeting of those interested in promoting a Fair for Cleveland County held on last Friday, the following officers were elected:

A. E. Cline, King's Mountain ... President
Lester Herndon, Grover ... Vice-President
George Blanton, Shelby ... Vice-President
Wm. Lineberger, Shelby ... Vice-President
Dr. J. S. Dorton, Shelby ... Vice-President

Besides perfecting the organization it was decided to employ an expert from Raleigh to superintend the erection of the buildings as well as to lay out the grounds to best advantage.

In addition to this committees were appointed to call on the people to raise the remainder of the money required.

The farmers are requested to begin to get ready for their exhibits this fall when everything will be in shipshape and ready to show the world just what Cleveland can do.

While we have had unusual prosperity on account of the bumper crops of cotton and the fine prices prevailing last fall still it is realized that cotton may take a tumble and that might mean tight times in the event that we depend on the fleecy staple altogether for the bulk of our money crop.

Therefore it is proposed to "mix it up," so to speak, and to encourage the raising of poultry and cattle and also to pay more attention to dairying. The county fair will help out along this line. By comparing grade of stock raised when exhibited in open competition with herds from other counties it is presumed that our farmers and dairymen will benefit thereby.

A county fair such as we will have will be worth thousands of dollars to the people of the county. It will also afford a gathering place where those interested may gather and discuss the merits of various grades of cattle for milk producing qualities or perhaps the right brand for beeves. Then too, a farmer from at Casar may give his brother farmer from Kings Mountain his experience with a certain kind of cotton seed that he had used during the season.

It is hard to estimate the value of the county fair to a community and Cleveland with $10,000,000 worth of various crops should set the pace for the state and there isn't a doubt in the world in our mind but that she will do it.

The March 18, 1924, issue of the *Highlander* announced the formal organization of the Cleveland County Fair Association, with A.E. Cline of Kings Mountain being elected association president. Lester Herndon of Grover, George Blanton of Shelby, William Lineberger of Shelby, and Dr. J.S. Dorton of Shelby were all elected vice presidents. County commissioners designated 46 acres from the County Home's property, centrally located on the Shelby–Kings Mountain Road, to be the home for the Cleveland County Fair. An expert from Raleigh was employed to help lay out the grounds and erect buildings. Farmers were asked to prepare to enter products for exhibit. (Image by Margaret Patterson.)

In the fall of 1923, the newly formed Kiwanis Club was looking for an event to sponsor. Under the leadership of club president O. Max Gardner, local attorney and later governor of North Carolina, the Kiwanis Club began brainstorming projects for consideration. It was noted that surrounding counties held county fairs, and the question was asked—why not Cleveland? Gardner and Odus Mull are credited with writing the association's bylaws. (Courtesy of Madge Harris.)

Local veterinarian Dr. J.S. "Doc" Dorton (center) accepted the daunting task to plan and organize the first county-wide fair. In only six months, Doc oversaw the construction of the grandstand, racetrack, and livestock barn with exhibit halls. Little did Doc realize that this venture was the start of a 38-year career of managing the Cleveland County Fair.

Here is a rare image of the original grandstand as it looked in the 1920s. From the fair's inception, the grandstand attracted large crowds for stage show revues and horse races.

The arched entrance to the massive stone grandstand is seen in this 1940 photograph. The stone grandstand was built in 1935 with help from the WPA (Work Progress Administration) and housed two levels for exhibit halls and offices. The Shelby Bus Line ran a special bus from uptown Shelby to the front gate of the fair.

An aerial view of the fairgrounds shows the 46-acre tract leased to the fair association by the county commissioners. Top center of the image shows the County Home, and to the top right is the Cleco Dairy Farm.

An image from the early days of the fair shows the midway and grandstand. Millers Brothers Shows were the first carnival attractions signed to appear at the Cleveland County Fair.

This 1949 image of the livestock barn shows the massive size of the structure. The center section with the dome top served as the show arena.

A rare image from the 1920s shows the barns before the show arena was added to connect the two buildings. One of the livestock barns was originally used as an exhibit hall.

A close-up view in the show arena demonstrates the healthy exchange between competitors. While each one hopes his entry will place first, they admire the entries from their friends and neighbors.

A large crowd gathers for the judging of dairy cattle. The community prides itself on improvements that have been made in this area since the competition started. Dairy farming was a large contributor to the economic development of the county.

Back in the exhibit hall, great care is taken by judges comparing contestants' entries in jellies, jams, and preserves. Being chosen best by one's peers is a great honor.

Improved canning practices were developed through friendly competition. This impressive display presents the county's finest. The many ribbons denote winners in their respective categories.

The farm exhibit from the Bethware community celebrates improved yields from better farm practices. This is a win for the entire community.

The Arey Oil Company went to great lengths to prepare its 1948 exhibit with gas pumps, tires, and batteries. The ceiling to the exhibit is slanted, as the exhibit hall is located under the grandstand seating.

Fairgoers pack the grandstand in anticipation of an upcoming motorcycle race. Zeb V. Cline used teams of mules and "drag pans" to build the racetrack.

From the fair's inception in 1924, horse races were a very popular attraction. Horse racing remained popular for another 20 years and was eventually replaced by rodeos and auto races.

Indy-style race cars prepare for the next event as fans in the infield watch prerace activities on the stage. The livestock barn is seen in the distance behind turn No. 2.

The 4,200-seat grandstand provided an excellent view of the half-mile racetrack. Those in the box seats were able to experience the race on a more personal level, as they usually went home covered in a fine layer of dust.

Just inside the front gate at the entrance to the grandstand sits a specially prepared stunt car from the "Lucky" Teter thrill show. For decades, thrill-show promoters parked their cars near the front gate to attract fairgoers to attend their events.

Doc Dorton poses with Earl "Lucky" Teter. Teter, the daredevil who coined the phrase "hell drivers," began his automotive thrill shows in 1938. (Courtesy Mrs. J. Sib Dorton Jr.)

As one of his stunt drivers races a motorcycle through a wall of fire, "Lucky" Teter is seen to the left in his signature white shirt and pants with black boots.

"Lucky" Teter's Hell Drivers were known for their signature ramp-to-ramp car jump over a bus. Unfortunately, "Lucky" lost his life in such a jump in 1942.

The fair train has arrived in this 1946 image. The train cars of the World of Mirth Shows were transferred to sidetracks from the Southern Railway for unloading. The World of Mirth Shows had replaced the Johnny J. Jones Expo Shows as the carnival attraction.

The James E. Strates Midway train is being unloaded along Morgan Street. Locals would line the streets to get a glimpse of the show's trailers and animals as they paraded through town and out Marion Street to the fairgrounds.

The World of Mirth Shows provided the carnival rides for only two years. The three giant Ferris wheels were a highlight of the fair.

The James E. Strates Midway shows included an elaborate circus. Note all of the trailers used to transport the carnival exhibits and exotic animals to the fairgrounds.

The stone grandstand burned on Christmas Eve 1951. Arson was suspected but never proven. The devastation was felt by the entire community.

The exhibit halls and offices were completely destroyed in the fire.

Only the stone walls remained as the ashes continue to smolder the morning after the fire.

Not to be deterred, Doc used soil from the racetrack infield to cover over the ruins and make a natural incline with which to build the new grandstand. The stone wall facing the track remains intact today.

The Cleveland County Fair Association Board of Directors poses for this June 27, 1953, picture. They are, from left to right, (seated) Elbridge Weathers, Reverend Brock, Dr. J.S. Dorton, Tom Cornwell, Dr. E.B. Lattimore, and Odus Mull; (standing) Norman Lee, Sam Lattimore, Boyd Harrelson, Wayne Ware, and J.U. Rollins.

The fair staff is busy at work in this September 18, 1956, image. Identified staff include Ruby Surratt, Margaret Willis, Ruby Putnam, Charles McBrayer, and Louie Sellers.

Two

"Drivers, Start Your Engines."

"Drivers, start your engines" and horses, mules, camels, and ostriches. For nearly 50 years, the racetrack at the Cleveland County Fair hosted races of all kinds—harness horse races, Indy-style race cars, local hobby racers, Grand National stock cars, and yes, even camel and ostrich races. Edwin H. Cline is pictured manning a team of mules in a pulling contest in 1941.

Harness racing was a popular attraction for nearly 20 years at the Cleveland County Fair. Horses and professional drivers traveled to compete in Shelby. On occasion, local drivers would try their hand at horse racing to the delight of the local crowd.

Here is an up-close look at a racehorse, driver, and sulky by the livestock barn. In this era, drivers had to be quite skilled, as the carts did not have modern-day independent suspension.

In 1956, Gene Holter brought his racing ostriches and wild animal show to the fair. The show included ostrich racing on sulkies and ostriches versus trotting horses. Note the drivers using brooms in an attempt to motivate and steer the ostriches.

The Holter show also featured camel races. Local celebrities were coaxed into jockeying the animals. The wild animal exhibit reportedly included the world's only zonkey, half zebra and half donkey.

Indy-style racers became a popular attraction in the 1940s. Fans have packed the grandstand and stage alike as the racers take the green flag.

The grandstand is filled to capacity as a racer kicks up a cloud of dust from the red clay track. Note the simple wooden guardrail that was intended to protect spectators from the race cars.

While race cars are being unloaded from trailers, prerace acrobatics take place on the stage by the grandstand.

Racers take the checkered flag in a 1948 race. Note how race crews stand by the side of the track without regard to safety. In the background is the framework for fireworks that would cap off the evening's entertainment. Fireworks have always marked the end of the day at the Cleveland County Fair.

The poster announces that Jack Kochman's Hell Drivers will be in town for an afternoon performance. Promoter Jack Kochman put on automobile thrill shows for more than four decades before his retirement in 1989. Kochman's Hell Drivers performed at the 1964 World's Fair, putting on 1,200 performances. (Image by Margaret Patterson.)

Jack Kochman's Hell Drivers perform a crossover ramp jump. In the background, the stage has been prepared for an elaborate show.

A star with Jack Kochman's Hell Drivers for many years was Shelby native George Patton. Patton was known for spending as much time in the air as he did on the ground.

Believe it or not, even Crosleys were used by stunt drivers. Crosleys were subcompact cars that were built in the United States from 1939 to 1952.

Local drivers competed in the highly competitive Hobby Racing Association. Ben Dixon (No. 7), Tommy Eskew (No. 44), Preston Humphries (No. 114), and Daniel Warlick (No. 81) prepare for a race at the Cleveland County Fair. (Courtesy of Charles Webb.)

Local racers Ray Thompson (No. 81), Daniel Warlick (No. 98), and Preston Humphries (No. 114) battle in door-to-door competition in the early 1960s. In 1965, Warlick competed in several Grand National races. (Courtesy of Charles Webb.)

Roger Ware (No. 43), driving a 1962 Petty blue Plymouth that was previously raced by Richard Petty, and Charlie Blanton (No. 0) are pictured in a rare 1960s image. While racing purists will recognize that this action was captured at Rutherford Speedway, both racers were regulars at the Cleveland County Fair. (Courtesy of Howard Scruggs.)

Local driver Gene "Stick" Elliott made the successful transition from hobby racing to racing in the Grand National series. Elliott competed in 93 Grand National races between 1962 and 1971.

July 26, 1956, marked the first Grand National race held at the Cleveland County Fairgrounds. The race promoter was Bruton Smith, who would later become president of Charlotte Motor Speedway.

Team owner Carl Kiekhaefer checks lap times with team drivers (from left to right) Herb Thomas, Buck Baker, and "Speedy" Thompson. (Courtesy of Shane Combs.)

"Speedy" Thompson won the first Grand National stock car race held in Shelby on July 26, 1956, driving a Dodge 500 similar to this car on display in the Chrysler Museum. Buck Baker won the October 23, 1956, race in a Kiekhaefer Chrysler 300. "Fireball" Roberts was first to the checkered flag driving a Ford at the May 4, 1957, race, and Buck Baker won for a second time in Shelby by taking the September 21, 1957, race in a Chevrolet.

A parade of beauty queens was a part of the September 18, 1956, prerace activities at the fairgrounds.

This is a close-up view of a beauty queen riding in the back of a 1956 Buick.

The pace car (a station wagon) leads the Grand National convertible division down the front stretch on a pace lap on September 18, 1956. This was the only Grand National convertible race held at the fairgrounds.

Joe Weatherly and Curtiss Turner take the green flag from flagman Roby Combs Sr. Turner won the 185-lap race, claiming the $500 purse in September 1956.

Ned Jarrett won both of the stock car races held at the Cleveland County Fair in 1965, taking $1,000 for the race on May 27 and an additional $1,000 for the race on August 5. Jarrett went on to win the 1965 Grand National drivers' championship. (*Racing Pictorial* photograph.)

Richard Petty finished second to Jarrett in the August 5 race. These were the last professional stock car races held in Shelby. (*Racing Pictorial* photograph.)

Three

The Stars Come Out

The fair already had the reputation of being one of the best in the nation. Residents of the county came together to showcase their best in agriculture, livestock, and home goods and were rewarded by the best the entertainment world had to offer. Emmett Kelly Jr., seated second from the right, is entertained in 1963 by fair officials including Elbridge Weathers, Bob Schafner, Otis Meachum, Jimmy Strates, Edwin Ford, Earl Meachum, and Fred Garland before Kelly's headline appearance in 1963.

Perhaps the most well-known and beloved clown in history, Emmett Kelly Jr. appeared at the Cleveland County Fair in 1963. Reprising the character created by his father, "Weary Willie," Kelly was a beloved mime best known for the famous "Sweeping the Spotlight" routine at the end of his shows.

The year after Emmett Kelly Jr. appeared in Shelby, he became Eastman Kodak's representative at the New York World's Fair, becoming one of the top attractions in its two-year run. Kodak was so impressed with Kelly's success during the fair that the company asked him to become its touring ambassador of goodwill, visiting thousands of towns and hospitals throughout the United States.

Film actress and television star Faye Emerson cuts the ribbon at the opening ceremonies of the 1951 fair. Acting and starring in several Warner Bros. films in the 1940s, Emerson hosted her own talk-and-musical variety shows in the early 1950s and became known as the "First Lady of Television." She is pictured here with fair manager Doc Dorton and her husband, well-known bandleader Skitch Henderson.

Assistant fair manager E.L. Weathers interviews the 1948 Apple Queen, Patty Osborne Lee, along with Dr. Dorton. A native of Lawndale, Patty was also crowed Miss North Carolina later that year.

George A. Hamid Sr. and Jr. were father-and-son entrepreneurs who made major contributions to America's outdoor entertainment industry and were two of the booking agents for the Cleveland County Fair. After moving from Lebanon in the early 1900s, Hamid Sr. got his start working with the Buffalo Bill Wild West Show. Hamid Jr. was later known as the "King of the Boardwalk" after building a series of theaters in Atlantic City.

The 1957 fair is an example of the star-studded Hamid acts. Although Lassie and the Lone Ranger were the headliners, each act brought the thrill and glamour of the entertainment world to Cleveland County. On Broadway, the first fair manager, Doc Dorton, was known as "the man who could book the best, yet stretch the dollar further than anyone else around."

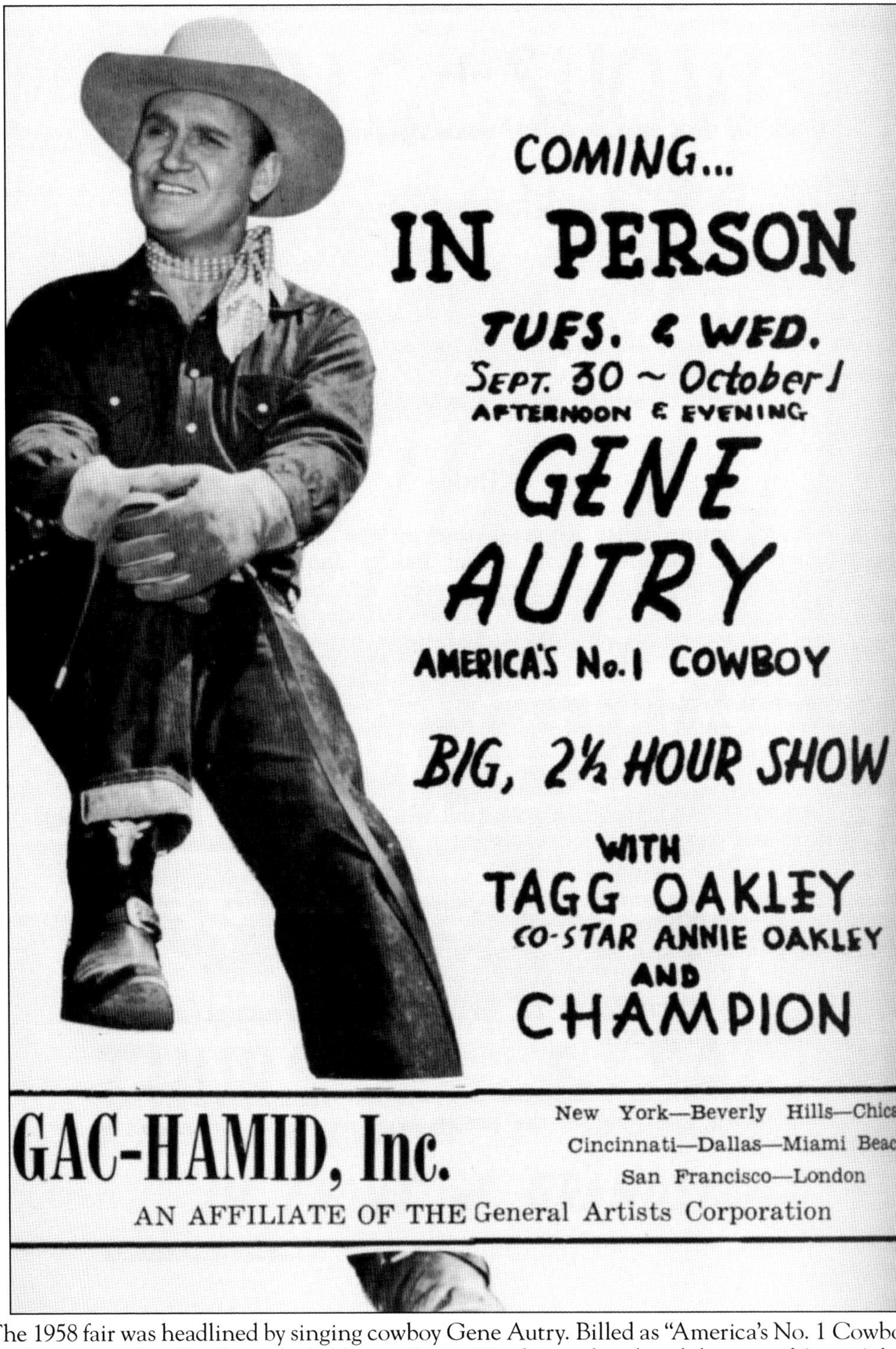

The 1958 fair was headlined by singing cowboy Gene Autry. Billed as "America's No. 1 Cowboy," he also appeared in Shelby with child actor Jimmy Hawkins, who played the part of Annie's little brother Tagg in the then-popular *Annie Oakley* television show. Jimmy was also featured as four-year-old Tommy Bailey in the motion picture *It's A Wonderful Life*.

Pictured with his horse Champion, Gene Autry is "back in the saddle again" at the 1958 fair. Autry gained his fame as a singing cowboy on radio, movies, and television beginning in the 1930s. Starring in more than 100 motion pictures, Autry made 640 recordings, including more than 300 songs he had written himself. He is credited with more than a dozen gold and platinum records.

Clayton Moore, as the Lone Ranger, and Jay Silverheels, as Tonto, appeared at the Cleveland County Fair in 1958. Star of the television series from 1949 to 1951 and again from 1954 to 1957, Moore trained his voice to sound like the star of the radio version of the *Lone Ranger*, which had aired since 1933.

Pat Boone, flanked by four armed bodyguards, arrives at the Cleveland County Fair in 1956. For a period in the late 1950s, he was second only to Elvis Presley in popularity and recording statistics. According to *Billboard* magazine, he still holds the record for having the most consecutive weeks on the charts with one or more hit songs.

Pat Boone's boyish good looks and old-fashioned values made him very popular in the early rock-and-roll era. Here is Boone (left) with Doc Dorton and two star-struck Shelby teenagers. According to an opinion poll of high school students in 1957, the singer was nearly the "two to one favorite over Elvis Presley among boys and preferred almost three to one by girls."

Fair manager Doc Dorton introduces Pat Boone to some of the finest Cleveland County Fair cuisine. One can only wonder if there was vinegar on those french fries.

Up close and personal, Pat Boone distributes autographed photographs to his fans in the grandstand. Note his signature white shoes.

Originally founded in 1925 and known as the "Missouri Rockets," this dance troupe was brought to New York by Samuel Roxy Rothafel to perform at his Roxy Theater and was renamed the Roxyettes. When Rothafel left the Roxy Theater to open at Radio City Music Hall, the troupe followed and was known as the Rockettes.

The Roxyettes, whether on stage in New York City or the grandstand at the Cleveland County Fair, were an instant sensation. They were the quintessential American chorus line—an exciting precision drill team with great style. They could do complicated tap routines with "eye-high kicks," promising to "knock your socks off."

The Cleveland County Fair poster featuring the famous Roxyettes shows a rather scantily clad dancer. While lavish and dazzling as promised, the troupe had a more family-oriented program on the stage. Because there were not enough hotels in the area, the Roxyettes stayed with local residents who lived in the community. (Image by Margaret Patterson.)

Billed as "something new under the sun," the Ice Variety Show featured a cast of 30, a six-piece orchestra, and a 35-by-70-foot ice tank. The colorful lights, dazzling costumes, wonderful musical scores, and choreography were usually something seen only in the biggest cities.

The 1974 fair brought the Geraldos, performing high-wire stunts and entertainment. In a thrilling death-defying feat, the young woman pictured here was unattended on the spinning wheel that was swinging back and forth on a giant pendulum.

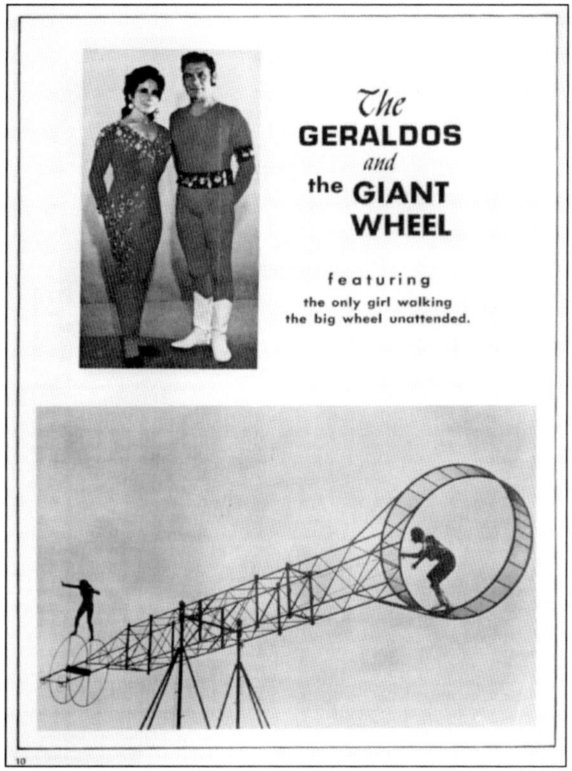

Originally part of the Ringling Bros. Circus, the Great Wallendas, consisting of Enrico Wallenda and his wife, Debbie, were a third-generation high-wire act who appeared at the fair in the early 1980s. Holding several Guinness World Records, the Wallendas offered a show of thrills, stunts, and theatrical entertainment that honored the traditions of their family's enterprise. Enrico's mother, Carla Wallenda, was a Cleveland County Fair favorite several years earlier.

In the 1950s, the fair was still segregated; however, African Americans were part of the featured entertainment in veteran Broadway showman Irving C. Miller's shows. Dubbed *Brownskin Models*, the show featured lighter-complexioned African American showgirls.

Miller's minstrel shows also featured popular blackface comedians, singers, dancing girls, and vaudeville entertainment. Many popular jazz and blues musicians got their start touring with Irving Miller's shows.

Irving Miller also owned the Rita Cortes burlesque show. Providing adult entertainment, dancing girls came out front to draw the crowds in. This particular show was called *Hawaiian Nights* and featured hula dancers with grass skirts.

In the 1960s and early 1970s, burlesque was still offered as popular entertainment at the fair. Sandy O'Hara at one time was considered the top fan dancer in the industry. After appearing at the fair in the late 1960s, O'Hara was bestowed the title of Miss Armed Forces Pinup by all five branches of the military during the Vietnam War and was featured in several television and movie roles.

Beauty queens and pretty girls have always been an important part of the Cleveland County Fair, as seen in this 1948 photograph. This young woman is entertaining the boys in uniform who are on leave to attend the fair.

Susan Proffitt Abercrombie, Miss North Carolina in 1976, is presented a bouquet of roses from Cleveland County fair manager Sam Goforth. Abercrombie, a Forest City native, was a special guest at the opening ceremonies in 1976.

"Sib" Dorton, Cleveland County fair manager, gallantly assists Maria Beale Fletcher, 1962 Miss America, at the carousel. Fletcher, an Asheville native, is to date the only Miss North Carolina who went on to claim the national crown.

Miss America Maria Beale Fletcher clutches her crown while she and her escort in suit and tie enjoy the Scrambler. Besides visiting the Cleveland County Fair, Fletcher did the usual tour visiting the troops in Germany, England, and France and even danced with Vice Pres. Lyndon Johnson at the Cherry Blossom Festival in Washington, DC.

Lassie, a fictional collie dog in the novel *Lassie Come Home*, became a cultural icon in the 1940s, 1950s, and 1960s after a dog named Pal assumed the stage name "Lassie" in a series of movies and television shows by the same name. Pal's owner and manager, Rudd Weatherwax appeared with Lassie at rodeos, fairs, and similar events in the early 1950s, including the Cleveland County Fair.

My Friend Flicka, a 1941 novel made into a trilogy of films in the 1940s, featured a young Roddy McDowall with Fred MacMurray. Flicka appeared at the Cleveland County Fair in the late 1940s with her foal, Thundersmoke.

Well-known Grand Ole Opry star Porter Wagoner appeared at the fair in the 1960s with a young woman he was introducing to the country-and-western world. Local radio disc jockey Charlie Cabaniss was introduced to the duo and even played a round of golf with them. Thinking she would not be around very long, Cabaniss never got the autograph of the young blonde—Dolly Parton.

Dr. Josip Marcans, touted as the one of the world's leading experts on tigers, was featured at the fair in the early 1980s. He began working with animals during his childhood in Croatia and later became a veterinarian. In the United States, he began breeding endangered Bengal tigers and founded a natural habitat reserve. In addition to touring with his tigers at the fair, Marcans made several appearances on *The Ed Sullivan Show*.

Josip Marcans Lions and Tigers
Adriatic Animal Attractions

Betty Feezor (right) was a beloved WBTV personality who had her own show from 1953 until 1977 featuring home cooking and decoration. Betty started working in Charlotte for 4-H clubs and the Girl Scouts while remaining a housewife, but it was not long before WBTV learned she was equally at home in front of a camera.

To generations of youngsters growing up in the greater Charlotte area, Fred Kirby was the friendly singing cowboy on a series of WBTV children's shows and the sheriff of Tweetsie Railroad. Influenced by yodeler Jimmie Rodgers and movie and recording star Gene Autry, his success started in the 1930s and 1940s, when he was also one of the area's most prolific radio and recording stars.

Tommy Faile, known for his guitar work, rich baritone voice, and snappy comedy routines, was a longtime member of the Crackerjacks band with Arthur, Sonny, and Ralph Smith. He appeared on WBTV's *Arthur Smith Show* beginning in the early 1950s and launched his own WBTV program, *The Tommy Faile Show*, in 1969; it ran until 1975.

George Lindsay (center), better known as "Goober Pyle" from the *Andy Griffith*, *Mayberry R.F.D.*, and *Hee-Haw* television shows, appeared at the Cleveland County Fair in 1998 and is pictured here with several local residents. Also known for his philanthropic efforts, he has raised over a million dollars for his home state of Alabama's Special Olympics.

Benny Koske, known as "Boom Boom Benny," has made a career of blowing himself up and reportedly has "loved every minute of it." Crawling into his homemade coffin and filling it with dynamite, Koske got his start as the human bomb in the early 1960s when he saw a stuntman blow himself up on television and determined that it was something he could do, making it even more interesting.

Making multiple appearances at the Cleveland County Fair during the 1960s and 1970s, "Boom Boom Benny" Koske is pictured here with fair manager Joe Goforth. In addition to being featured in fairs and races throughout the United States, Benny was a featured guest on more than one occasion on *The Tonight Show Starring Johnny Carson*.

Four

Agriculture Impacts Economic Development

Coinciding with the fall harvest, Wayne Ware Sr. displays apples from his King's Mountain farm at the 1940 fair. Showcasing the county's progressive agriculture and impacting local economic development, each of the managers, Dr. J.S. "Doc" Dorton (1924–1961), J. Sibley Dorton Jr. (1961–1962), Elbridge Weathers (1962–1973), Sam Goforth (1973–1976), Joe Goforth (1977–2004), William Edmondson (2005–2006), Fuchia Allen (2007–2009), and Calvin Hastings (2010–present), can be proud of their tenure.

These 1948 judges for jams, jellies, and marmalades take their job very seriously. Judges were especially instructed not to award premiums for any entry because of its presence, but each should be "individually worthy" and "possess high intrinsic merit."

Canned fruits and vegetables, jams, and marmalades are on display in the 1951 exhibit hall. Entries were judged on color, clearness, texture, ripeness, appropriate size and packing, and uniformity of containers and labels. Blue-ribbon winners in each category won $2 in prize money as well as the bragging rights of being known as the best in the county.

It was quite an honor to take home a blue ribbon from the Cleveland County Fair. The friendly competition had each homemaker working fervently throughout the year to perfect her special recipes. Here are the prize-winning cakes and pies from 1938.

The 1948 Exhibit Hall was decorated to celebrate the best the county had to offer in home goods, fruits and vegetables, arts and crafts, prize-winning farms, and educational displays. Commercial booths also displayed the best and newest equipment for homes and farms.

In 1941, Lattimore offered this display of farming practices in its community. Careful attention to detail showed the pride each entrant took both to produce and display his or her best.

During World War II, local communities were proud to display patriotic themes, knowing that, as local farmers, they were furthering the cause of common defense. They were part of the strength of this nation, providing food and soil reserves unequalled anywhere in the world.

Cleco Farms, located just beyond the front gate of the Cleveland County Fair, boasted 54 acres of permanent pasture orchard grass and clover, 57 registered Guernsey cows, and three fish ponds supplying water for pasture irrigation. Later, it was known as Carolina Dairy.

This 1956 display by, from left to right, Elijah, Arlene, and Roger Royster of Fallston shows their "Dream Farm and Home." In 10 years, they hoped to produce $10,000 net annual income from their laying hens. In addition to winning third prize for its exhibit, the Royster family won $40.

The Better Acres Program, sponsored by the Agricultural Workers Council of Cleveland County, was a very practical way of improving farming practices in the county in the 1940s and 1950s. Families who entered the program worked with the council on definitive ways they could improve their farming practices during the year.

Each family entering the Better Acres Program had a booth that displayed how its farm was at the beginning and end of the year. This booth was the John and Yates Hawkins display of their Boiling Springs farm in 1948. The best three booths won $75, $60, and $50—but every entry won at least $40.

Selected by the council as having made the most improvements during the year, the Better Acres Farm was awarded a $1,000 grand prize at a special ceremony on the grandstand. Farms were judged on soil conservation, efficiency of crop and livestock production, farm and home improvements and beautification, farm buildings and machinery, and time and effort each family put into the project as well as general interest and participation.

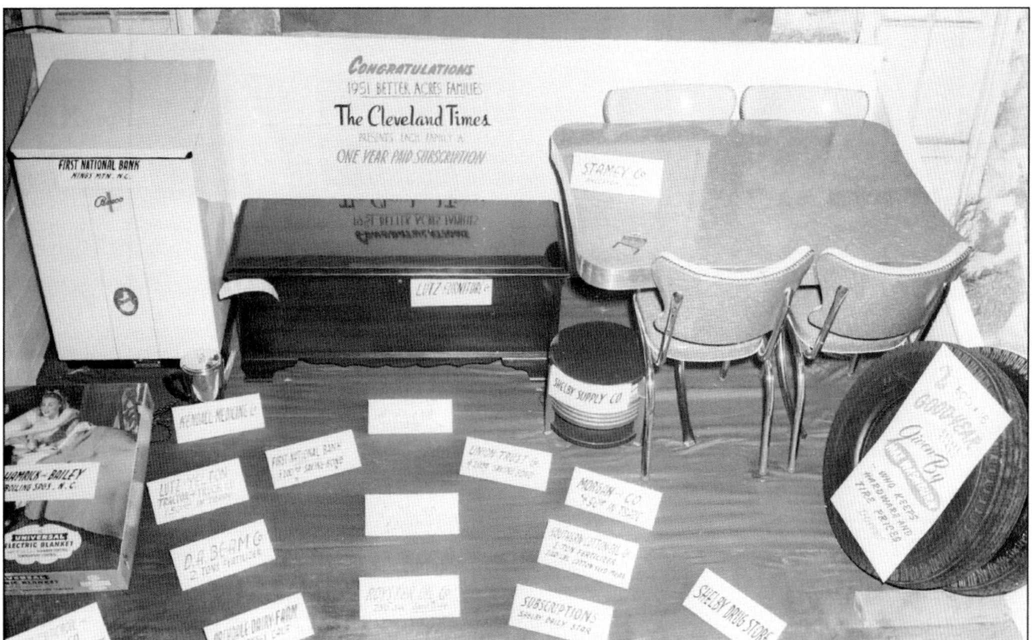

Other prizes, pictured here, were given by commercial firms in the county to all the Better Acres families for their participation. Besides the furniture, water heater, tires, electric blanket, and coffee pot seen here, each family received 3,000 pounds of fertilizer, two $100 savings bonds, a Guernsey calf, and $350 cash from anonymous donors.

From left to right, Doc Dorton, Mal Spangler, and an unidentified woman present prizes to two teens from one of the local 4-H clubs. A community-based development program for youth, 4-H focuses on values relating to head, heart, hands, and health to better equip the leaders of tomorrow.

This 1950 exhibit from Scout Troop No. 5 in Shelby celebrates the 40th anniversary of the Boy Scouts of America.

Each of the local schools provided exhibits to showcase important educational values. Here are local teens and their teachers preparing the school booths before the 1954 fair.

Casar School provided this exhibit at the 1938 fair. Students created a relief map of their community, showing local farms, roads, and industry.

Local radio station WOHS had this popular booth in the 1948 Exhibit Hall. Local musicians provided entertainment that was broadcast live from the fair.

Local businesses set up commercial booths to display the newest and best in home and farming equipment. These "modern" wringer washing machines at the Sterchis exhibit were very popular with homemakers attending the fair.

Imagine having nine lovely colors to choose from in the newest rotary telephones. The phones are almost as lovely as the young ladies with gloves, corsages, and tiaras displaying them.

Local service clubs were always involved in community projects. Here, a grand effort is made to raise money for cerebral palsy as the Elks Club sells raffle tickets to win this brand new 1954 Cadillac.

Before Miss Piggy, the Cleveland County Fair had KewTee, a glamorous piglet complete with bows and frills, shown here by Amy Cline Hull in 1964. Hull continues to participate in the fair each year, currently serving on the board of directors.

At the fair, one could count on seeing the biggest and the best in agriculture and livestock. The year 1938 was no exception, as this young farmer shows his prize hog named Hoov.

Marion Moss, a member of the Waco 4-H Club, is shown with one of her prize-winning roosters at the 1951 fair. Fairgoers were able to purchase many of the animals on display, and the young people used the proceeds to reinvest in animals to raise in the following year.

These two farmers are showing the Brahman cattle outside the livestock barn. Note the "Whip the Boll Weevil" sign on the side of the barn. The boll weevil had become a serious problem throughout the South, particularly in this county where so much cotton was raised.

Purebred cattle was unheard of in the early 1920s but soon became the norm as friendly competition at the fair brought about improved strains. This 1951 prize-winning heifer, with flowers and a bow, is almost as dressed up as the woman showing her. At that time, besides winning a blue ribbon, a first-place heifer could win a $10 cash prize.

Gov. Kerr Scott participates in the 1951 milking contest at the Cleveland County Fair. North Carolina's 62nd governor, Scott was a lifelong advocate for agricultural issues.

This 1940s photograph shows a young lad in knickers with his pony. At that time, ponies could be shown in the livestock barn but also entered in the pony races on Tuesday and Friday afternoons at the fair. Often, Cleveland County youngsters went on to compete in pony races at the state fair in Raleigh, bringing home prize money and championships.

Crowds gather as ponies are being shown in the livestock barn in 1956. First place would bring a coveted blue ribbon and a cash prize of $7.

This 1997 photograph shows a proud Matthew Brotherton with his grand champion pony Honeybee Stinger and the trophy they won.

Even the youngest cowboys take their work seriously at the Cleveland County Fair.

Five

The Magic Midway

With sawdust in one's shoes and the taste of cotton candy on the tongue, a fairgoer could prepare for the thrill of the roller coaster and Ferris wheel, anticipate the curious collection of sideshows, and settle down for a night of fun. The Cleveland County Fair is in town, and everyone knows magic can be found on the midway.

These four youngsters enjoy a ride on the ever-popular carousel at the 1952 fair. The little girls in the center of the photograph have come prepared for their adventurous pony rides, having donned their cowgirl hats.

Airplane rides, swings, roller coasters, and the Hollywood Midget Circus are only a few of the attractions on the midway in the 1950s.

By simply looking at the skull-and-crossbones flag on the lead car, fairgoers could sense the danger and adventure that awaited them on this 1948 roller coaster.

The Wall of Death was the original extreme motorcycle and small car thrill show, featuring a barrel-shaped wooden cylinder whose vertical walls daredevil drivers circled performing stunts. The roar of the engines and the vibrating rumble of the cylinder amazed spectators standing at the top of the barrel looking down, inches away from the drivers risking their lives.

What fair is complete without a treasured memento to remember the occasion? This young girl and her mother carefully choose a souvenir from a vendor on the midway in 1951.

Entertaining sideshows are also part of the fair's success. The racing monkeys featured "world championship monkey drivers," including crowd favorite "Mile-a-Minute-Murphy." The sign on the right reveals that the "big payoff" for first prize was $10,000 in monkey money or a stalk of bananas.

Very popular in the mid-1960s, the Skydiver Ferris wheel cars were mounted on a circular frame but spun on a front-back axis, like a barrel roll.

In 1961, a mobile chair lift, the Skyliner, developed by Shelby's Goforth Industries, was added to the mix of rides. From the lift's vantage point, one could view all the fair had to offer. The lift ran from the exhibit halls to the rear gate entrance to the grounds.

Part musician, part comedian, Panhandle Pete was an unforgettable entertainer who performed on the midway in 1954. A self-proclaimed "Poor Man's Philharmonic," Pete played 14 instruments, strapped to his body, in his one-man band. Besides touring fairs and festivals throughout the Southeast, he made guest appearances on television programs such as *The Ed Sullivan Show*.

This early-1960s photograph shows Beechnut's Tobacco-Spitting Contest and a very young contestant stepping up to the line. This scene would not be found at today's fair.

In 1952, a local dance team known as the "Wray-etts" was part of the free entertainment at the Cleveland County Fair. Pictured are, from left to right, Lynn Lutz, Betsy Lackey, Nancy Canipe, Becky Arey, Elaine Canipe, Margie Greer, and Cynthia Grice. The team was named after their dance instructor, Janie Cline Wray.

Appearing at the fair in the early 1970s, the Budweiser Clydesdales are a team of horses well-known for their commercials by the Anheuser-Busch Brewing Company. Standing 18 hands (6 feet) tall at the shoulder, this impressive breed was first made famous in 1933, when it was used in a ceremony to carry cases of beer to legislators after the repeal of Prohibition.

Unaware of the "Caution Wild Animals" sign in the background, a little girl makes friends with this elephant at the fair. In early fairs, elephants were unloaded on the fair train in uptown Shelby and paraded down Marion Street to the fairgrounds. Here, they performed in the free circus but were also used to set up the circus tents and push the trailers into place.

The Terrel-Jacob's Wild Animal Circus was featured at the 1952 fair. Under the big top, one could see dancing elephants, bareback riders, funny clowns, trained horses, jungle-bred lions, royal Bengal tigers, and hair-raising acts guaranteed to thrill people nightly. It took 45 railroad cars to bring the circus to town.

The Stebbing Royal European Circus was a mainstay of the fair in the 1970s. Here is Robert Stebbing holding the tiger Maya as fair manager Sam Goforth touches her head. His hand did not stay long, as the tiger whipped her head around and placed her teeth around Goforth's wrist. No injury was incurred, but it did take a while for Sam to recover the color in his face.

Children were still able to get up close and personal with exotic animals whenever the circus was part of the Cleveland County Fair. These youngsters enjoy an elephant ride before the show under the big top.

The World Championship Wild West Rodeo, under the direction of B.D. Adams, first appeared at the fair in 1954. The rodeo featured cowboys and cowgirls in stiff competition for big cash prizes and points toward winning the National Rodeo Championship.

A blend of performance and contest, the rodeo promised "wild outlaw bucking horses, fighting bulls, clowns, comedians, stunt drivers and trick riding," a real taste of the Old West.

Pretty cowgirls joined the competition in trick riding, barrel racing, and goat tying.

This young performer was a particular inspiration to the local youth who longed to be cowboys and cowgirls themselves.

Wearing their finest dresses, these young ladies choose candy apples at one of the many concession stands in the early 1960s. It was always appropriate to dress up for special occasions, and nothing was more special than the Cleveland County Fair.

Staples of fair cuisine have always been peanuts, popcorn, and cotton candy. One can always satisfy a sweet tooth at the fair.

Shelby Lions Club had a concession stand to benefit charity in 1940 that featured a 12-ounce bottle of Double Cola or Nehi for a nickel or 32 ounces of the beverage for 10¢.

Jaycees also had a concession stand. In this 1948 picture, it is obvious that the fair was a very popular place for soldiers on leave.

The Deggeller office wagon and workers are pictured in this mid-1960s photograph. Troupes that have played at the fair include the Miller Brothers (1924), Johnny J. Jones Expo Shows (1925–1930), Rubin & Cherry Shows (1931–1937), Setlin & Wilson Show (1938), World of Mirth Shows (1946–1947), James E. Strates Shows (1948–1962), Deggeller Shows (1963–1975), and Reithoffer Shows (1976–present.) The fair was closed during World War II, from 1942 to 1945.

In 1940, there was a local crew to direct traffic and park cars. Members did such a great job that they were asked to also work at the state fair in Raleigh. Pictured are, from left to right, Gillette Hamrick, Jake Anthony, unidentified, Gus Anthony, Boyd Camp, and Bunyan Jones.

A day at the fair always ended with a spectacular display of fireworks. For many years, the local Bost Bakery sponsored the nightly event at 10:00 p.m. The conclusion of the display was the signal for kids to head to the car; it was time to go home.

Volunteers have always been an important part of the fair. Many from the community work year round, coming together to make sure everything is in working order as the Cleveland annually hosts the biggest agricultural county fair in the state.

Cleveland County's public servants have always been an important part of the fair. Here are local policemen and firemen who volunteered to help at the fair. On the front-right bumper of the fire truck is Knox Hardin, chief of police.

Ever mindful of the Cold War, local policemen demonstrate gas masks and show the community some of the weapons in their arsenal. There was also a bomb shelter near the waterwheel that one could tour.

A familiar face in law enforcement in the 1950s was Sgt. J.B. Kuykendall, who spent his career with the North Carolina Highway Patrol. Uniformed highway patrolmen have always used the fair as a vehicle to meet and greet the public and keep them aware of safety.

Master trooper Phillip Glover talks with fair participants about safety in this 1980s photograph.

A young Marion Patterson Lee enjoys one of the kiddie rides at the fair in the 1980s. The fair has always featured a special "Kiddieland of Rides," built on a small, extra-safe scale, just like the ones mom and dad used to enjoy.

Since its introduction at the 1893 World's Fair in Chicago, no fair is complete without the magic of a Ferris wheel. The Deggeller Magic Midway featured two side-by-side Ferris wheels as well as the double Ferris wheel at the 1971 fair. Not only can passengers see the lights and action of the entire fairground from this high vantage point, but also, young couples often steal a kiss or two while on the Ferris wheel.

Since the mid-1980s, pig races have become a popular attraction at the fair. Crowds gather at the "Hogway Speedway" to cheer for their favorite porker. The "swine master" introduces the celebrity contestants (usually named after stock car favorites), assigning cheering sections for each piglet, and a special cheerleader from the audience for each section. The winning piglet gets a plate of cheese puffs, and the cheerleader gets the coveted blue ribbon.

In Shelby, the name "Bridges" has long been associated with mouth-watering barbecue. Here, Ken Bridges is in front of a barbecue stand by the same name. Ken was a brother of Red Bridges, who owned Bridges Barbecue Lodge.

Local middle and high school cheerleaders are involved each year in friendly competition to be known as the best in the county. Crest High School cheerleaders are pictured in the 1993 competition.

Jane Campbell's Dance School performed "The Little Teapot" at the 1998 fair. Pictured are Sydney Hush, Elainie Cass, Shantel McGill, Ashley Gillmore, Brooke Jones, Kelsey Terry, Dakota Martin, Mikalia Butler, Whitney Terry, and Victoria Powell.

Still performing today, the Frank Love Orchestra was featured at the Performing Artists of Cleveland County (PACC) stage in 1996. The PACC stage showcases local entertainment each year.

This 1990s image shows the Crest High School marching band performing at the fair's opening ceremonies in front of the Dorton Exhibit Hall. Using local talent continues to celebrate the fact that this is Cleveland County's fair.

Three young cowboys stand at attention during the national anthem before the rodeo in 2003. Rodeos at the fair always begin with the national anthem. These young cowboys patriotically stand at attention as the American flag is brought into the arena.

Since its introduction at the 1954 fair, the rodeo has been a popular attraction. Pictured above is the bull-riding competition in the year 2000.

After years of hosting visiting beauty queens, in 1987, the fair decided to crown its own. Jill Hamrick Martin was crowned the very first Miss Cleveland County Fair.

In later years, motocross events at the Cleveland County fairgrounds were added. This photograph was taken in 2003.

Helen Borders is one of the many volunteers who make the fair a success year after year. Borders, along with the rest of her family, spent her childhood working at the fair and stayed involved "because it was a good community project and good, clean fun." One of the many projects she has been involved with over the years is the annual Miss Cleveland County Fair contest.

Joe Goforth (second from right) is inducted into the International Association of Fairs and Expositions Hall of Fame in 2006 after serving as fair manager for 27 years. He is pictured here with former managers Fuchia Allen and Bill Edmonson and Joe's wife, Sophia (right). Born the year the fair started, Goforth attended every fair during his lifetime.

Six

It's a Brand New Day at the Cleveland County Fair

The Cleveland County Fair celebrated its 87th anniversary in 2011 with such stars as the JaneDear Girls, the Travis Powell Band, and Elvis Presley tribute artist Ryan Pelton. The image above demonstrates the excitement of the fair through the eyes of a young girl on the merry-go-round. (Photograph by Scott Glover.)

Cleveland County Fair Association Board chairman Andy Elmore (left) and fair manager Calvin Hastings (right) tour the midway during the 2011 fair. With the 2010 hiring of Hastings as fair manager, the board of directors has brought a new level of enthusiasm to the fair. Hastings said, "We have come a long way since 1924 and have a long way to go. We have lots of plans for our Cleveland County Fair to make it bigger and better each year."

Ambrose Cline is pictured with his wife, Jean, and daughter Amy Cline Hull during the 2011 fair. Ambrose and Charles Beam were recognized with the distinction of having attended every Cleveland County Fair since its beginning in 1924.

Agriculture exhibits and competition remain healthy components of the annual fair. Blue-ribbon winners continue to enjoy bragging rights of being the county's best. (Photograph by Scott Glover.)

Public schools throughout the county prepare exhibits for judging each year. The theme from Jefferson Elementary was "The Track for Success Begins with Education."

The Peeler log cabin exhibit is a great example of an 18th-century Cleveland County home. The log cabin has been a permanent part of the fair since 1973.

The fair partners with local churches to host a nondenominational church service each year. Pictured above is the crowd that gathered in the Weathers Arena for the Sunday morning service in 2011 with Elizabeth Baptist Church hosting.

From left to right, Andy Elmore, Ashley Bridges, and Will Thompson look on as the livestock judge prepares for the next competition.

The expression on young Renee Bridges's face reflects the excitement during the judging process. (Photograph by Scott Glover.)

A Bandy High School student leads a shorthorn cow from Zac Loman's farm during the parade of animals for judging.

Black Angus cattle, bred primary for beef production and known for their superior quality, line up with their owners before the panel of judges.

In the junior division, young girls show their sheep in hope of winning the blue ribbon. Keeping the sheep in the circle is often a daunting task, particularly with the distraction of the crowds.

Dairy goats have become a popular addition over recent years at the fair. The barn in the background has been decorated with artistic renditions of the animals it houses.

A view of the carnival rides demonstrates the size of North Carolina's largest agricultural county fair. To the left is the Piedmont Shriner booth. A trip to the fair is not complete without a ham biscuit from the Shriners. (Photograph by Scott Glover.)

The Cullers French Fries stand is an institution at the fair. Fairgoers debate whether they use vinegar or not on their fries. (Photograph by Scott Glover.)

Here is a view of a crowded local food stand. A wide variety of foods is available, including Knobby Burgers. Many of the food vendors today are from Cleveland County. The fair is an excellent venue for local restaurants to reach a wider audience of consumers. (Photograph by Scott Glover.)

A vendor's trailer advertises elephant ears. Through the years, funnel cakes have grown in popularity, replacing the elephant ears. (Photograph by Marie Patterson.)

Bingo has been a regular attraction at the fair for over 70 years. This is probably the most popular game of chance offered at the fair. Prizes include the usual stuffed animals as well as useful household items. (Photograph by Scott Glover.)

The Fat Albert game of chance has been a fan favorite for decades. Contestants bet on the color of the cubby hole that they think Fat Albert (the rat) will run to. (Photograph by Scott Glover.)

A new attraction to the 2011 fair was a trout-fishing catch-and-release pool. This young lady was particularly proud of her catch of the day. (Photograph by Scott Glover.)

A fan favorite for generations has been the water-gun balloon game. The object is for contestants to be the first to burst the balloon with water shot from the gun. (Photograph by Scott Glover.)

Carnival rides are a major attraction at the fair. Here the Orbiter is in the foreground, in front of the Zipper and the ever-popular Ferris wheel. (Photograph by Scott Glover.)

Squeezing into the seat next to one's best friends and screaming as the ride dips and whirls is all part of the experience of riding the Tornado. (Photograph by Scott Glover.)

Bungee jumping, modified for its youngest riders, can be enjoyed by all ages at the Cleveland County Fair. This young man enthusiastically recoils into the air, delighting in the experience and ready to go again. (Photograph by Scott Glover.)

The roller coaster continues to be a major part of the carnival rides on the midway. The downhill scream is part of the fun. (Photograph by Scott Glover.)

A recent addition to the fair is the mechanical bull. The operator can adjust the bull to suit a rider's ability. (Photograph by Marie Patterson.)

For decades, another fan favorite has been the bumper cars. These young enthusiasts take pleasure in crashing into their siblings and friends. Who needs driver's ed? (Photograph by Marie Patterson.)

The fair conducts cheerleader competitions for high school and middle school students. The cheerleading squad from Crest High School performs on the grandstand during the finals.

The Burns High School cheerleading squad competes on the grandstand as competing squads watch on.

Award-winning country music stars Susie Brown (left) and Danelle Leverett of the JaneDear Girls perform at the 2011 fair. Describing themselves as "feminine, All-American and country," the duo electrified the Cleveland County crowd.

Ryan Pelton is an Elvis Presley tribute artist. Pelton's performance is unique in that his concert includes songs throughout Elvis's career from the 1950s to his Las Vegas shows.

As night falls, the fair is transformed into a "City of Lights," as illustrated in this aerial photograph. (Photograph by Scott Glover.)

Fireworks have been a part of the fair since its inception and indicate the end of the fair day. (Photograph by Scott Glover.)

The Cleveland County Fairgrounds have become a popular venue for attractions throughout the year, including the Hog Happnin', Christmas at the Fair, Spring Garden Show, and the weekly farmers' and flea market. Every November, the Home Builders Association sponsors the Hog Happnin' barbecue-cooking contest. Cooking teams from across the Southeast compete in the annual event.

Pictured above is a close-up view of a contestant's cooker. Contestants know that barbecue is a staple in Cleveland County, and great care is taken to produce that perfect flavor.

Barbecue-cooking teams submit their entry at the judges' table. After judging is complete, participants as well as the local community enjoy a wonderful barbecue dinner.

Other events at the Hog Happnin' include a car show, concerts by local favorites, and a craft fair. Not unlike the competition with farm animals at the county fair, the cars are lined up and engines on display as owners compete with their neighbors for the best in show.

Tractor pulls, known as one of the world's most powerful motor sports, have been added to the annual event at the fairground. Tractors are pitted against a weighted sled pulled along the dirt track.

Pickup trucks are as popular in Cleveland County as barbecue, so it was only natural to add a truck pull to the 2011 Hog Happnin'.

Monster truck competition is back by popular demand at the fairgrounds. Contestants are judged on their best time while crushing anything in the truck's path.

The demolition derby continues to be a fan favorite on the grandstand. As competition gets underway, the spectators in the background will be covered with a fine layer of red clay from the famous Cleveland County Fair dirt track.

Christmas at the Fair returned to the fairgrounds in 2011. The waterwheel is decorated for the holiday season.

Christmas at the Fair features an exhibit competition, decorations, and a wide variety of craft and retail vendors.

The American Legion World Series Committee booked the fairgrounds for an exciting kick-off to the 2011 American Legion World Series. More than 6,000 fans jammed the grandstand for the Ronnie Dunn concert. Baseball teams, fans, and legion officials from across the United States were on hand for the concert.

Country music singer-songwriter Ronnie Dunn performs at the fairground. Dunn, known as half of the duo Brooks and Dunn, began working as a solo artist in 2011. One of the most consistently successful acts on the circuit, Brooks and Dunn sold over 30 million records with 20 No. 1 singles. At this writing, they have won more Academy of Country Music awards than any artist in the history of country music.

Discover Thousands of Local History Books Featuring Millions of Vintage Images

Arcadia Publishing, the leading local history publisher in the United States, is committed to making history accessible and meaningful through publishing books that celebrate and preserve the heritage of America's people and places.

Find more books like this at
www.arcadiapublishing.com

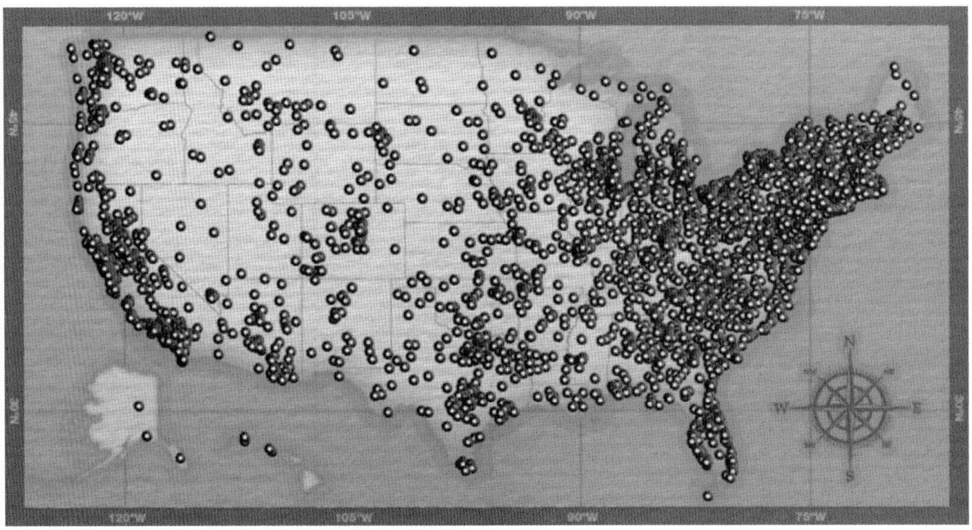

Search for your hometown history, your old stomping grounds, and even your favorite sports team.

Consistent with our mission to preserve history on a local level, this book was printed in South Carolina on American-made paper and manufactured entirely in the United States. Products carrying the accredited Forest Stewardship Council (FSC) label are printed on 100 percent FSC-certified paper.

MADE IN THE USA